a litt

Celtic
wisdom

compiled by sean mcmahon

illustrated by jon berkeley

First published in 1995 by
The Appletree Press Ltd
The Old Potato Station
14 Howard Street South
Belfast BT7 1AP
Tel: +44 (0) 28 90 243074
Fax: +44 (0) 28 90 246756
E-mail: reception@appletree.ie
Web site: www.appletree.ie

A Little Book of Celtic Wisdom

The acknowledgements on page 4 constitute
an extension of this copyright page.

A catalogue record for this book is available
from the British Library

ISBN 0-86281-561-4

CONTENTS

ACKNOWLEDGEMENTS

The publisher wishes to thank the following for permission to reproduce copyright material:

Brandon Book Publishers for quotations from *A Golden Treasury of Irish Poetry*.

Paul Carney for the quotation by James Carney.

Devin-Adair, Publishers, for the translations by Robert Macalister and Eoin MacNeill, and F.N. Robinson (copyright by Devin Adair, Publishers inc., Old Greenwich, Connecticut, 06870. Permission granted to reprint quotations from *Old Irish Sources* by Macalister and MacNeill and from *1000 Years of Irish Poetry* (1947) by Kathleen Hoagland. All rights reserved.)

Oxford University Press for the quotations from *The Irish Tradition* (1947) by Robin Flower and *Early Irish Hymns* (1970) by Gerard Murphy (by permission of Oxford University Press).

Penguin Books Ltd for the quotations from *The Mabinogion* translated by Jeffrey Gantz (Penguin Classics, 1976) copyright © Jeffrey Gantz, 1976, reproduced by permission of Penguin Books Ltd.

Peters, Fraser and Dunlop for the extract from *Kings, Lords and Commons* by Frank O'Connor (reprinted by permission of the Peters, Fraser and Dunlop Group Ltd).

Routledge for the quotations from *A Celtic Miscellany* by Kenneth Hurlstone Jackson.

While every effort has been made to contact copyright holders, the publisher would welcome information on any oversight which may have occured

I NTRODUCTION

Long, long ago, beyond the misty space
Of twice a thousand years,
In old Erin there dwelt a mighty race,
Taller than Roman spears.

Such was the rather romantic description of the Celts by the nineteenth-century poet, Thomas D'Arcy McGee. In fact the Celts preferred farming to fighting, but they did have iron, which was equally useful for swords and ploughshares. They originated in central Europe and moved east and west to leave their influence on all European teritories except the Mediterranean. The Greeks knew them as Keltoí and they met the Romans often in battle as the dreaded Gauls. Their Roman adversaries were always greatly impressed by their eloquence, and the aforementioned D'Arcy McGee by their tales told of high deeds and their wonderful wooing of very emancipated women.

Of all the Celtic languages, Irish probably has the richest store of literature. The hero-tales,  which had hitherto been preserved orally, came to be written down by the Irish monks whose métier was essentially the writing down of knowledge. What began as the transcribing of Latin came to include vernacular copying. Celtic lore, both pagan and Christian, was preserved in a series of magnificent "Books" which were produced in the twelfth century, but which contain both poetry and prose from earlier periods. In other Celtic countries too, particularly in Wales, the Isle of Man, Scotland and Northern France, the old tales were preserved monastically.

This little selection tries to present something of the Celtic temper. While not being quite the wild romantics that some have painted them, the

Celts have and always did have a sense of spirituality, of nature and the year's changing, of conviviality, of mocking humour and, most of all, a rage to express themselves in talking and writing about all these things. They  impressed the Romans enough to make them popular as tutors of the children of the aristocracy and now, over two millennia later, they may reasonably claim that, in their own expression, they "never lost it."

ROUGH WINTER HAS GONE

Delightful is the season's splendour,
Rough winter has gone:
Every fruitful wood shines white,
A joyous peace is summer.

*from "Song of Summer",
Irish, 9th century, version Meyer*

Greetings to you gem of the night!
Beauty of the skies, gem of the night!
Mother of the stars, gem of the night!
Foster-child of the sun, gem of the night!
Majesty of the stars, gem of the night!

"To the Moon",
traditional Scots Gaelic, version Jackson

Green bursts out on every herb;
The top of the green oakwood is bushy.
Summer has come, winter has gone,
Twisted hollies wound the hound.

"Summer",
Irish, 10th century, version Meyer

The fish of Ireland are a-roaming,
There is no strand which the wave does not
pound,
Not a town there is in the land,
Not a bell is heard; no crane talks.

from "A Song of Winter",
Irish, 10th century, version Meyer

My tidings for you: the stag bells,
Winter snows, summer is gone.
Wind high and cold, low the sun,
Short his course, sea running high.

from "Summer Is Gone",
Irish, 9th century, version Meyer

Keen is the wind, bare is the hill, it is difficult to
find shelter; the ford is marred, the lake freezes,
a man could stand on a single stalk.

from "Winter",
Welsh, 11th century, version Jackson

The winter is cold, the wind is risen,
The brave stag is on foot.
The whole mountainside is cold tonight
But the bold stag is belling.

from "The Colloquy of the Ancients",
Irish, 12th century, version O'Grady

I cannot sleep, I cannot leave the house, I am
distressed because of it. There is no world, no
ford, no hillside, no open space, no ground
today. I won't be tempted out of my house into
the fine snow on the word of a girl.

Dafydd ap Gwilym, c.1325–c.1380,
Welsh, version Jackson

Stumbling I turned
aside into a wide
swamp, a place very
like Hell, where a hun-
dred grinning goblins
were in every gully; I
could not find, in that
hellish marsh, a space
not choked with tan-
gled scrub. I shall not
go trysting again in the
wide mist—I am too
timid!

*from "The Mist",
attributed to Dafydd ap
Gwilym c.1325–c.1380,
Welsh, version Jackson*

Before God, my lass, I must make my way;
The whole land, every dale and glen, weeps its
long sorrow after the graceful summer; no tree-
top can do more, nor weep leaves after that.

Thomas Nicholson,
Welsh, 19th century, version Jackson

Gaily they grow; the
quiet throng, the fair
gems of the realm of
sun and wind; the
hanging bells of the
high crags, flowers of
the rocks, like cups
of honey.

"Heather Flowers",
Eifion Wyn
(1867–1926), Welsh,
version Jackson

Bitter is the wind
tonight,
It tosses the ocean's
wild hair;
Tonight I fear not
the fierce warriors
of Norway
Coursing on the
Irish Sea.

Irish, 8th century,
version by Meyer

"Who's that outside
With fear in his voice
That is battering my closed door?"
"I'm Ned of the Hill
Who is soaking and cold
From eternal prowling of mountain and glen."

from "Ned of the Hill",
Irish, 18th/19th century, version McMahon

All the sweetness of nature was buried in black
winter's grave, and the wind sings a sad
lament with its cold plaintive cry; but oh, the
teeming summer will come, bringing life in its
arms, and will strew rosy flowers on the face
of hill and dale.

from "Winter and Summer",
Thomas Telyong Evans, 1840–65,
Welsh, version Jackson

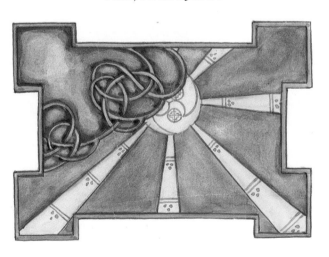

Sweet Was My Intimacy

I am Liadin
That loved Curither:
It is true as they say.

A short while I was
In the company of
    Curither:
Sweet was my intimacy
    with him.

The music of the forest
Would sing to me when
    with Curither:
Together with the voice of
    the purple sea.

*from "Liadin and
    Curither",
Irish, 9th century,
version Meyer*

Do you remember the night when you and I
were under the blackthorn tree, and the night
freezing? A hundred praises to Jesus that we did
nothing harmful, and that your crown of maid-
enhead is a tree of light before you!

Irish, traditional, version Jackson

There is one on whom I would gladly gaze, to whom I would give the bright world, all of it, all of it, though it be an unequal bargain.

"Gráinne Speaks of Díarmait",
Irish, 9th century, version Murphy

Great love of a man from another land
Has come to me beyond all else:
He has taken my bloom, no colour is left,
He does not let me rest.

from "The Song of Crede, Daughter of Guaire",
Irish, 10th century, version Meyer

Everything new is neat – cheers! A young man is changeable in his desires, lovely are decisions about love and sweet the words of a man who comes wooing.

from "The Book of Leinster",
Irish, 12th century, version Greene & O'Connor

...my love is reckless and loudly boastful, and rashness will lead men astray. I spent a third of the night in great anxiety on a most miserable journey, to get a kiss from my generous sunny-hearted girl, since I had her consent.

Attributed to Dafydd ap Gwilym c.1325–80, Welsh, version Jackson

Tell him it's all a lie
I love him as much as my life;
He needn't be jealous of me
I love him and loathe his wife.

Irish, 15th century, version O'Connor

There is a youth
comes wooing me;
oh King of Kings,
may he succeed!
Would he were
stretched upon my
breast, with his body
against my skin.

*Isobel, Countess of
Argyll, Scots Irish, 15th
century,
version Jackson*

And I said I would not sell it for a hundred
pounds nor a hundred loads, nor for the fill of
two meadows of oxen with their yokes, and for
the fill of St David's churchyard of herbs trod-
den out; that was the way I would keep the shirt
of the lad I loved best.

Welsh, 16th century, version Jackson

Gold wears out, silver wears out, velvet wears
out, silk wears out, every ample garment wears
out – yet longing does not wear out.

Welsh, 17th century, version Jackson

It's well for you,
blind man, who see
nothing of women!
Ah if you saw what
I see you would be
sick like me. I wish
to God I had been
blind before I saw
her curling hair, her
lithe and slender
snowy body; ah, my
life is full of pain.

Uilliam Ruadh c.1690–1738, Irish, version McMahon

24

Do you remember when you and I lay at the rowan's foot while the night grew deadly cold? We had shelter from neither wind nor rain except my coat beneath us and your gown about us.

*from "The Coolin", Irish, 18th century,
version McMahon*

O, that the great sea would dry up to make a
way, that I might go through: the snow of
Greenland shall grow red like roses before I can
forget my love.

Manx, traditional, version Jackson

Often you and I sported, while the others
searched for us, till we chose to return to the
meadow where the calves were.
We on the hill crest, my arms around your neck,
listening to the chorus in the tops of the
branches.

"The Braes of Glen Broom"
attributed to William Ross, 1762–90, Scots Gaelic,
version Jackson

I'd wed you without cattle, without money,
without dowry itself,
And I'd kiss you of a dewy morning at
daybreak.
It is my sickness sore that we are not together in Cashel, O love of my heart,
Even though a plank of plain bog-deal made
our bed.

from "Cashel of Munster",
Irish, 18th century,
version O'Donoghue & McMahon

Whiter than the breast of a white swan were her two breasts; redder than the foxglove were her cheeks. All who saw her became filled with love for her. Four white clover flowers would grow up in her footprints wherever she went; and hence she was called Olwen ("white footprint").

Welsh, 10th century, version Jackson

She's my pulse, she's my secret, she's the scented flower of the apple, she's summer in the cold time between Christmas and Easter.

Irish, 18th century, version Jackson

CALLED A HOME

The fort over against the oak-wood:
Once it was Bruidge's, it was Cathal's,
It was Aed's, it was Aillil's,
It was Conaing's, it was Cuiline's,
It was Maeldúin's:
The fort remains after each in his turn—
And the king asleep in the ground.

Irish, 5th century, version Meyer

My little lodge in Tuaim Inbir—
There's no great house of statelier timber;
With its stars at evening bright,
Sun by day and moon by night.

Irish, 8th century, version Robinson

I invoke the land of Ireland.
Much-coursed be the fertile sea;
Fertile be the fruit-strewn mountain;
Fruit-strewn be the showery wood.

from "Invocation to Ireland"
(The Book of Invasions), Irish, 12th century,
version Macallister & MacNeill

Endlessly over the water
Birds of the Bann are singing;
Sweeter to me the voices
Than any church bell's ringing.

from "The Madness of Sweeney",
Irish, 12th century, version O'Connor

Were all Alba mine
From its centre to its border,
I would rather have the site of a house
In the middle of fair Derry.

It is for this I love Derry,
For this quietness, for its purity,
And for the crowds of white angels
From one end to the other.

from "Columcille's Greeting to Ireland",
Irish, 12th century, version Reeves

Earth that is heaviest with the fruit of trees,
Earth that is greenest with lushest grass,
Old plain of Ir, moist and fertile,
Wheaty, branchy land.

from "Farewell to Fál [Ireland]",
Uilliam Nuinsean, 1550–1625,
Irish, version McMahon

Lovely to be on the Hill of Howth, truly delightful to be above its white sea; an opulent fertile
hill, abounding in ships, a headland rich
in wine and warriors.

Irish, 14th century, version McMahon

I was in service for a while near Ty'n y Coed,
and that was the most delightful place I was
ever in. The little birds were warbling, and the
trees were murmuring together—but my heart
poor in spite of all those.

Welsh, 17th century, version Jackson

Long the road and wide the mountain from
Cwm Mawddwy to Trawsfynydd, but where a
lad's desires may lead him the hill seems a
descent.

Welsh, 17th century, version Jackson

O fair sweet princess, if it is your destiny to be
my love,
Give me your solemn promise before I travel
with you to the west:
If I die by the Shannon, on Man's isle or Egypt
the grand,
Let it be with the wholesome Irish people of
Creggan that I am laid to rest.

from "The New Churchyard at Creggan",
Art Mac Cumhaidh, 1738–73,
Irish, version McMahon

Fine is the clothing of Craig Mhór—there is no coarse grass for you there, but moss saxifrage of the juiciest covering it on this side and on that; the level hollows at the foot of the jutting rocks, where the primroses and delicate daisies grow, are leafy, grassy, sweet and hairy, bristly, shaggy—every kind of growth is there.

from "The Misty Corrie",
Duncan Bán MacIntyre, 1724–1812,
Scots Gaelic, version Jackson

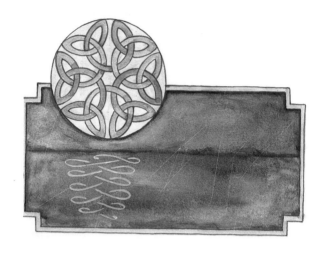

The dim night is silent, and its darkness covers
all Snowdon; the sun in the bed of the sea, and
the moon silvering the flood.

Gwalter Mechain, 1761–1849,
Welsh, version Jackson

Now with the coming of spring the day is lengthening and after the feast of Brigid I'll hoist my sail. Since I've taken the notion I'll not bide until my feet are set in County Mayo. It's in Claremorris I'll rest the first evening and in Balla below I start on the drink; I'll head for Kiltimagh and spend a good month there, and that's not a league from Ballinamore.

from "Killeden", Antaine Ó Reachtabhra, 1784–1835,
Irish, version McMahon

With a cup of beer and a morsel to eat,
We shall live as safely as the farmers in peace;
Let us heartily drink to our own company,
Among men we're cheerful, though following
the net.
Now to put an end unto what I have said,
May plenty of herring be in Mann for aye;
Keep for us the blessing, O world's Creator,
And let the Manx people with thanks open
their mouths.

*from "Song of the Herring",
Rev. John Cannell, 1798–1810,
Manx, version Moore*

SPELLS AND ENCHANTMENTS

Across the sea will come Adze-head
crazed in the head,
his cloak with hole for the head,
his stick bent in the head.

He will chant impiety
from a table in front of his house;
all his people will answer:
"Be it thus. Be it thus."

"Adze-head",
Irish, 7th century, version Carney

Four times three, three times
four, fit for every need,
Twice six in the church, both
north and south—
Six pairs besides myself,
Praying for ever the King that
makes the sun shine.

from "The Hermit's Song",
Irish, 9th century, version Meyer

It was in April that Eilleen returned and spring
came back to the Isle of Man, and it has been so
ever since, for each year the princess brings life
to the flowers in the spring and they fade when
she leaves in the autumn.

"The Bride of Elfland",
traditional Manx fairy tale, version Falconar

Kei [Sir Kay of Arthur's Round Table] had this talent: nine days and nine nights his breath would last under water, and nine days and nine nights he could go without sleep. No doctor could cure the wound from Kei's sword. He could be as tall as the tallest tree in the forest when he pleased while, when the rain was heaviest, what was in his hand would be dry by reason of the fire he generated, and when his companions were coldest that would be kindling for the lighting of the fire.

from "The Mabinogion",
Welsh, 14th century,
version Gantz

And then they took the flowers of the oak-trees
and the flowers of the broom and the flowers of
the meadowsweet, and out of these they created
the fairest and most perfect girl that man has
ever seen. And they baptized her by the baptism
they used in those days, and called her
Blodeuwedd [flower-face].

Welsh, 11th century, version Jackson

As for the third plague, a mighty magician is carrying off your food and drink from the banquet table. His spells and enchantments cause everyone to fall asleep, so you will have to stand watch yourself—lest sleep overcome you too, have a vat of cold water close by, and when you feel sleepy step into the vat.

from "Lludd and Llevelys" (The Mabinogion), Welsh, 14th century, version Gantz

You are the lovely red rowan that calms the wrath and anger of all men, like a wave of the sea from flood to ebb, like a wave of the sea from ebb to flood...

Scots Gaelic,
From a traditional charm, version Jackson

B E THOU MY VISION

I arise today
Through the strength of heaven;
Light of sun,
Radiance of moon,
Splendour of fire,
Speed of lightning,
Swiftness of wind,
Depth of sea,
Stability of earth,
Firmness of rock

from "The Deer's Cry",
attributed to St Patrick,
Irish, 7th century,
version Stokes, Strachan & Meyer

It's evil
to shun the King of righteousness
and make compact with the demon.

"God and the Devil",
Irish, 7th century, version Carney

God's blessing lead us, help us!
May Mary's son veil us!
May we be under His safeguard tonight!
Whither we go may he guard us well!

Noah and Abraham,
Isaac the wonderful son,
May they surround us against pestilence,
That famine may not come to us!

from "Hymn against Pestilence",
attributed to St Colman, Irish, 8th century, version
Stokes and Strachan

Be Thou my vision, O Lord of my heart,
Naught is all else to me save that Thou art.
Thou my best thought in the day and the night,
Waking or sleeping, Thy presence my light.

from "A Prayer",
Irish, 8th century, version Hull

To go to Rome—
Is little profit, endless pain.
The Master you seek in Rome
You find at home or seek in vain.

Irish, 9th century, version by Meyer

May no demons, no ill, no calamity or terrifying
dreams
Disturb our rest, our willing prompt response.
May our watch be holy, our work, our task,
Our sleep, our rest without let, without break.

"Patrick Sang This",
Irish, 10th century, version Meyer

Shame to my thoughts, how they stray from me!
I fear great danger from it on the day of eternal
Doom.

During the psalms they wander on a path that is
not right:
They fash, they fret, they misbehave before the
eyes of the great God.

Through eager crowds, through companies of
wanton women,
Through woods, through cities—swifter are they
than the wind.

from "On the Flightiness of Thought",
Irish, 10th century, version Meyer

Jesus be thanked, to a foreign country here have I come; I will go on shore—Lord Jesus, kind heart, guide me to a good place that I may worship my dear Christ and Mary the virgin flower. I have come to land and am weary with travelling. Mary, mother and maid, if you have house or mansion near here, guide me to it, for indeed I should greatly wish to make me an oratory beside Mary's house.

from "St Meriasek Comes to Cornwall"
(from the miracle play "Beunans Meriasek"),
Cornish, 15th century, version Jackson

Weariness of the legs after some active deed is better than apathy and weariness of spirit; weariness of spirit lasts for ever, weariness of the legs lasts only for an hour.

Scots Irish, 15th/16th century, version Jackson

Generation by Generation

Whether morning, whether evening, whether by land or sea, though I know I shall die, alas, I know not when.

Irish, 9th century, version Jackson

What I have loved from boyhood I now hate – a girl, a stranger, and a grey horse; indeed I am not fit for them.
The four things I have most hated ever have met together in one place: coughing and old age, sickness and sorrow.

from "Senility", attributed to Llywarch Hen, Welsh, 9th century, version Jackson

Once I was in the grove, sick for the sake of my bright girl, composing a love-charm, a brilliant snatch of song, on a day of sweet sky at the beginning of April...Haughty and sharp-beaked, from the thorn thicket the Magpie muttered a querulous grumble: 'You fret yourself much with your worthless bitter song, all to yourself, you aged man! Better for you, by Mary of eloquent words, to be by the fire, you old grey man than here among the dew and rain in the green grove and the cold shower.'

from "The Magpie's Advice",
Dafydd ap Gwilym, c.1325–c. 1380,
Welsh, version Jackson

As in the season of ice there are caught in the snares birds seeking their food, and fish in nets, and none so much as dreamed till now of dying, yet now they are prepared for supper over the charcoal fire; so is your life, from beginning to end, which you pass in the world, always among sins, and if you do not amend them before the end of your days after all your pleasures, you will stay in the snares...

"Damnation", Mestre Jehan an Archer Coz,
Breton, 1519, version Jackson

When a man is past forty, though he flourishes like the trees in leaf, the sound of a vault being opened makes his face change.

Welsh, 17th century,
version Jackson

Alas I have no longer the
gift of sight;
In lonely pride I cannot
see the young leaves grow
Nor can I still in good
company go to hear
The sweet song of the
cuckoo at the forest's
edge.

from "Welcome to the Bird",
Séamas Dall Mac Cuarta, c. 1650–1733,
Irish, version McMahon

It is grief to me that after the toil of battle they
suffered the agony of death in torment, and a
second heavy grief it is to me to have seen our
men falling headlong; and continual moaning it
is, and anguish, after the fiery men lying in the
clodded earth...

from "The Gododdin", attributed to Aneirin,
Welsh, 5th century, version Jackson

Into his grave, and he is gone, no more talk
about him; earth's crop, which generation by
generation slips away into oblivion.

Ioan Arfon, 1828–81,
Welsh, version Jackson

She died, like the gleam of the moon when the
sailor is afraid in the dark; she died like a sweet
dream when the sleeper is sad that it has gone.
She died, at the beginning of her beauty;
Heaven could not dispense with her; she died,
oh Màiri died, like the sun quenched
at its rising.

"The Death of Màiri", Evan Maccoll, 1808–98,
Scots Gaelic, version Jackson

The youth do not believe that age will come;
The old do not believe that death will come.

Scots Gaelic proverb, version McMahon

A man fair of face
was here yesterday;
now he is nothing
but blood beneath
clay.

*from "The World",
Irish, 11th century,
version Carney*

Yellow bittern, it grieves me sore that you lie
With your bones strewn about, picked clean;
It wasn't lack of food but drouth
That left you flattened there.
I think it worse than the fall of Troy
That you lie stretched on naked flags,
You who caused neither harm nor woe
And ever preferred marsh water to wine.

*from "The Yellow Bittern",
Cathal Buí Mac Giolla Ghunna, c.1680–1755,
Irish, version McMahon*

ENDURING IN THE LIGHT OF DAY

I and Pangur Bán, my cat,
'Tis a like task we are at;
Hunting mice is his delight,
Hunting words I sit all night...

Practice every day has made
Pangur perfect in his trade;
I get wisdom day and night
Turning darkness into light.

from "The Monk and His Cat",
Irish, 9th century, version Flower

A hedge of trees surrounds me,
A blackbird sings to me;
Above my lined booklet
The trilling birds chant to me.

In a grey mantle from the top of the bushes
The cuckoo sings:
Verily—may the Lord shield me!—
Well do I write under the greenwood.

"The Scribe",
Irish, 9th century, version Meyer

My hand is weary with writing,
My sharp quill is not steady,
My slender-beaked pen pours forth
A black draught of shining dark-blue ink.

from "Colum Cille the Scribe",
Irish, 11th century, version Meyer

God of heaven does not disturb me in my high
marvellous poetry; he pours freely the beauty of
red gold over my utterances.

"The Poet",
Irish, 12th century, version Greene & O'Connor

Though this is a poem of close-knit lore, I have walked all over Munster with it, every market-place from cross to cross—and it has brought me no profit from last year to the present.

"Who Will Buy a Poem?", Mathghamhain Ó hIfearnáin, c.1580–c.1640, Irish, version Jackson